IMAGES
of America

STEVENS POINT
BREWING COMPANY

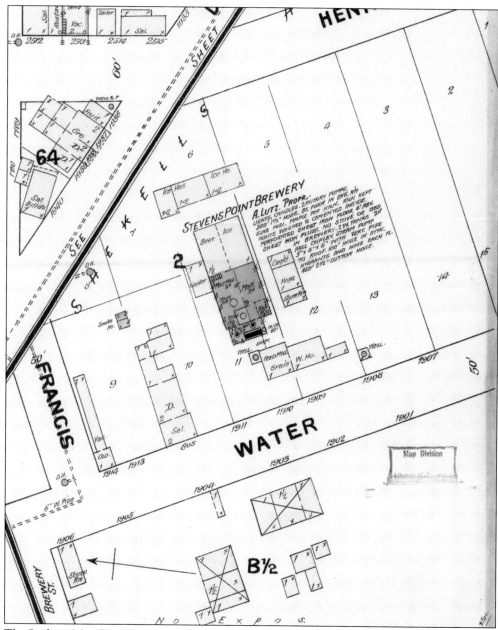

The Sanborn Map Company created fire insurance maps from 1867 to 1961 for insurance companies to assess liability for properties. This is a Sanborn map from 1891 showing the Stevens Point Brewery under the ownership of Andrew Lutz. As Sanborn maps are known for their detail, this map shows the main brewery structure as well as other buildings on the site that housed ice and hops. In the bottom left of the map, there is a building marked "D." for dwelling and "Sal." for saloon. This building was the brewery storefront and home where the brewmaster's family lived. (Courtesy of the Library of Congress.)

ON THE COVER: Truck driver Victor Marshall is pictured here in the 1940s. Marshall drove delivery trucks for Stevens Point Brewery for 36 years, retiring in 1977. He passed away in 1987 at the age of 72. (Courtesy of the Portage County Historical Society.)

IMAGES
of America

STEVENS POINT
BREWING COMPANY

John Harry

ARCADIA
PUBLISHING

Copyright © 2019 by John Harry
ISBN 978-1-4671-0402-9

Published by Arcadia Publishing
Charleston, South Carolina

Printed in the United States of America

Library of Congress Control Number: 2019940811

For all general information, please contact Arcadia Publishing:
Telephone 843-853-2070
Fax 843-853-0044
E-mail sales@arcadiapublishing.com
For customer service and orders:
Toll-Free 1-888-313-2665

Visit us on the Internet at www.arcadiapublishing.com

To Rikki, who is constantly challenging me to
be my best self and follow my dreams

CONTENTS

Acknowledgments   6

Introduction   7

1.   Beginnings   11

2.   Incorporation   23

3.   Survival   43

4.   The Best Beer in America   87

5.   The Next Chapter   119

About the Organization   127

ACKNOWLEDGMENTS

This book would not have been possible without the assistance and patience of these individuals: Rikki Harry, University of Wisconsin (UW)-Milwaukee professor Chris Cantwell, UW-Stevens Point professor Sarah Scripps, Brad Casselberry, Dana Hansen, Lee Reiherzer, John Zappa, Ken Shibilski, Joe Martino, Julie Birenkott, Brian Elza, Art Oksuita, Kevin Knitt, and many others.

There were also several organizations that were essential in making this book a reality: the Stevens Point Brewery, Portage County Historical Society, University of Wisconsin–Stevens Point Archives, Almond Historical Society, Marquette County Historical Society, Marathon County Historical Society, and South Wood County Historical Society.

Finally, a huge amount of gratitude is owed to the people of Stevens Point. The enthusiasm they hold for their beer and its past was a key motivator in finishing this project. Their pride in their community makes Stevens Point a wonderful place to learn and grow. No matter where I live, I will always be proud to call Stevens Point my hometown.

Unless otherwise noted, images in this book appear courtesy of the Portage County Historical Society.

INTRODUCTION

The first building in Stevens Point was a lumber storehouse. The second was a tavern. Before they built a bank, a general store, or even a schoolhouse, the people of Stevens Point established a place where they could share a drink and each other's company.

This culture of drinking had deep roots. Before the area had even been settled by Anglo-European pioneers, thirsty lumbermen journeying between Grand Rapids (now Wisconsin Rapids) in the south and Big Bull Falls (now Wausau) in the north stopped at failed lumber baron George Stevens's lumber storehouse to resupply, rest, and have a drink. Stevens's time in the locale that would bear his name was brief. However, his name would be connected to the identity of the people who came after him as a place to live, thrive, and survive.

In no case is this truer than with the city's long-standing brewery, the Stevens Point Brewing Company. As the fifth oldest brewery in the United States, the Stevens Point Brewery, commonly shortened to just Point Brewery, has survived not in spite of being located in a small town in north-central Wisconsin, but because of it. The loyalty of the people of Stevens Point toward their brewery and the brewery's loyalty to them in return has been unchanging and unwavering.

With German immigration to Stevens Point in the 1850s came a staple of their diet: lager beer. While beer had been transported to Stevens Point before the surge of German immigration in the 1850s, that beer was more likely to be an ale. Ales use yeast that can ferment at room temperature and be aged in the bottles or kegs that they will be consumed from. Lager yeast ferments at colder temperatures and requires a 6–10 week lagering period in cold storage. Lagering is a notable German method of brewing, and it is certainly more difficult to make due to the necessity of temperature control.

German immigrant George Ruder sought to capitalize on the thirsty population of Stevens Point. Ruder was born in 1827 in Nuremberg, Bavaria, and learned how to brew at his father's brewery. He immigrated to Milwaukee in 1854 and worked at breweries there until 1856, when he decided to move north to start his own brewery in Stevens Point. In Stevens Point, Ruder came together with another German immigrant, Franz Wahle. By Christmas of 1857, Ruder and Wahle were brewing both lagers and ales, making 1857 the founding year of what would become the Stevens Point Brewery.

As the brewery was founded a year before the city was incorporated in 1858, the two entities have long been seen as linked. The growth of the city in the 1860s led the brewery to increase its capacity. This happened when then owner Andrew Lutz constructed a new stone brewhouse in 1872 to replace the original wood structure built by Ruder and Wahle. The stone structure still exists today within the larger complex that Point Brewery has constructed around it, much like the city has changed and evolved around the brewery itself.

During Andrew Lutz's ownership of the brewery from 1867 to 1897, people started referring to it as the Stevens Point Brewery. This surely put other competitors at a disadvantage as no one else could lay a stake to the claim that their beer represented the city. Lutz also was the first to call his beer "Special Beer," a moniker that years later resulted in the brewery's flagship brand being called Point Special.

When Lutz sold the brewery in 1897 to Bohemian immigrant Gustav Kuenzel, he did so to a person who understood that to be successful with the Stevens Point Brewery, one also had to be a supporter of the Stevens Point community. Kuenzel did this through helping to finance the building of the clock tower on Stevens Point's north side. He was active in causes associated with his involvement in the Independent Order of Odd Fellows, a fraternal organization that Lutz was also a member of. Kuenzel also kept up the brewery's standards by updating equipment and expanding the brewhouse again to keep up with the demand of Stevens Point residents.

Kuenzel's one folly happened in 1901, when he renamed the brewery as Kuenzel's Brewery, dropping any named association with Stevens Point. This was surely not taken kindly by Stevens Point residents who had come to calling the brewery their own. The brewery did not last long under this name, however, as Kuenzel sold the brewery to a group of local businessmen that year, possibly to leave town and restart his brewing career.

The group that bought the brewery from Kuenzel was made up mainly of well-known Stevens Point citizens, plus one outsider. The outsider was Michael Littel, a brewer from Green Bay. Wanting to buy a brewery but lacking the capital to do so, Littel found willing business partners in Stevens Point. Prominent members of the syndicate included hardware store owner Alexander Krembs, tavern keeper John Martini, and a former sales agent for Milwaukee's Pabst Brewing named Nicolas Gross. The group incorporated as the Stevens Point Brewing Company in October 1901.

The new brewery management undertook massive expansion for the brewery both in 1901 and again in 1907. At that point, the brewery was responding to increased demand as well as a formidable local competitor in the newly formed Polish Brewing Company. Point Brewery hired famed brewery architect Richard Greisser to design the updated complex, giving the brewery its distinct outline that lasted until further expansion in the 1990s and 2000s.

The Stevens Point Brewery also made a critical hire for brewmaster in 1912 when they brought George Egenhoefer onboard. It was Egenhoefer that led the brewing operations through Prohibition and established the modern version of Point Special. Egenhoefer served in the brewmaster capacity until 1944. From 1912 to 2011, only three different brewmasters led Point Brewery. This consistency in product quality is another reason for the brewery's longevity.

The brewing industry was given a major blow with the enactment of Prohibition laws in 1920. The brewery survived by making soda and near-beer, but Prohibition did not cause the city of Stevens Point to go dry. There were several local illegal liquor operations and a network of speakeasies in town. The soda fountains that served liquor had a telephone system where when one establishment got caught, the rest of the network would be warned, and everyone would chip in on the fine for the place that was first apprehended.

Sometimes, Point Brewery would "forget" to remove the alcohol from their near-beer, Point Special Beverage. A notable instance of this included a reunion of Spanish-American War vets. Around the time the brewery was packaging this illegal beer, state inspectors dropped by, which forced the brewery to take the beer and have it dumped out in back to avoid being caught. However, for every bottle a worker dumped out, a bottle was consumed. Apparently, there were many drunk Point Brewery employees stumbling home later that day.

Two instrumental families joined Point Brewery during Prohibition: the Korfmanns and the Shibilskis. Ludwig Korfmann bought the brewery in 1924, gambling that someday Prohibition would end and his investment would pay off. Korfmann hired Felix "Phil" Shibilski in 1930 as a manager. Between 1924 and 1995, either a Korfmann or Shibilski was always involved with Point Brewery. Again, this consistency was paramount in gaining consumer loyalty through more tough times to come.

When Prohibition ended in 1933, Point Brewery went back to doing what they did best: making beer. While sales increased drastically at first, output plateaued just as the nation was entering World War II. With wartime rationing in effect, Point Brewery dropped its less profitable products and put all of its efforts into making and marketing Point Special Lager.

Another setback to the company came in 1941, when Ludwig Korfmann passed away. This gave control of the brewery to Ludwig's son Calvin and daughter Estelle Ehlert. Calvin, as president of the brewery, was charged with the difficult mission of keeping the brewery in business. During the war, as other parts of the country were going through beer shortages, Point Brewery focused on their local market. People from Chicago offered Korfmann and Shibilski large amounts of money for Point Beer, which they always turned down. This loyalty to the people of Stevens Point would be reciprocated, as the brewery had more tough times ahead.

By 1970, most small, regional breweries like Point Brewery either were closed or close to shutting down. Large breweries were consolidating these smaller operations to increase their market share. Point Brewery might have followed suit if it was not for a fateful newspaper article that turned into a promotional bonanza.

In 1973, syndicated *Chicago Daily News* columnist Mike Royko put on a blind taste test of beer from all over the world. Coming in second place internationally, and first place among American beers, was Point Special Lager. Suddenly, people from all over the country wanted to try Point Beer, a beer that was only distributed in a 50-mile radius from Stevens Point at the time. Offers of distribution from around the country began streaming in, including one from Trans World Airlines that wanted to feature Point Special Lager on flights by ordering 200 cases per week.

Unsure if the brewery could keep up with the sudden added demand, Phil Shibilski and his newly hired son Ken turned them down. They wanted to ensure that the people of Stevens Point could always have their beer first, before anyone else. If the rest of the world wanted Point Special Lager, they would have to come to Stevens Point.

It was not until 1990 when people farther flung finally got their wish, and the brewery started distributing outside of Wisconsin. Since then, Point Brewery has continued to expand. While the brewery today would be nearly unrecognizable to its founders, the loyalty that has kept Point Brewery in business since 1857 continues to survive in the beer that Pointers call their own.

One

BEGINNINGS

When New Yorker George Stevens maintained his lumber storehouse at a small point in the Wisconsin River in 1839, few would have guessed that it would spawn a small settlement, never mind a bustling city with a vibrant downtown, university, and a brewery bearing Stevens's name. The beginnings of Stevens Point were indeed humble and, like Stevens, driven by the lumber boom of mid-19th-century northern Wisconsin.

By 1857, what had become known as Stevens Point had grown considerably and was one year away from being incorporated as a city. The population of Stevens Point had grown from 600 in 1853 to 2,000 in 1857. Due to the lumber trade, many of these new arrivals and temporary residents were European immigrants, specifically from Germany. In 1856, one of these German immigrants, George Ruder, arrived in Stevens Point after having spent the two years prior brewing in Milwaukee. Ruder purchased a brewery that was already under construction on the outskirts of Stevens Point on the Plank Road, now known as Water Street. In 1857, Ruder was joined by another German immigrant, Franz, or Frank, Wahle. On Christmas Day 1857, the *Wisconsin Pinery* reported that Ruder and Wahle were in business, making beer for the thirsty residents of Stevens Point.

At some point in 1860, Ruder and Wahle separated. Ruder moved north to Wausau and founded his own brewery there. Wahle, meanwhile, continued on his own. In 1862, German immigrant Jacob Lutz began apprenticing at the brewery. He was joined by his brother Andrew after the Civil War. In 1867, the Lutz brothers bought Wahle's brewery. When Jacob Lutz moved to Grand Rapids, Wisconsin, in 1880, Andrew Lutz continued brewing with his son John serving as brewmaster in the later years. In 1897, two years before his death, Andrew Lutz sold the brewery to Gustav Kuenzel.

The early years of the brewery solidified it as the Stevens Point Brewery, linking the brewery to the city.

In 1838, pioneering lumberman George Stevens stopped at a small point on the Wisconsin River on his way to Big Bull Falls (now Wausau). It was on this point that he constructed a storehouse, which led to the area being referred to as Stevens Point thereafter. Other than that small storehouse, Stevens has very little connection to the city that now bears his name.

George Stevens was not alone in his pursuit of the riches of the lumber trade. Thousands of settlers, many of them immigrants, came to Portage County in the mid-1800s as a result of the lumber boom. The river drivers in this picture are using spears known as "pike poles" to free a logjam in Northern Wisconsin.

Portage County, where Stevens Point is located, was a major beneficiary of the logging industry. As the lumber industry grew, so did the population of the county. This only intensified as the railroad reached Portage County in the early 1870s. From only hundreds of residents in the 1850s to around 25,000 residents by 1890, Portage County had established itself as a major hub in Northern Wisconsin.

As Stevens Point grew in the 1850s, more industry was needed to supplement the settlers arriving in the area. Newspaper advertisements were published in major cities like Milwaukee to request that members of certain service industries move to the area. Teachers, doctors, and clergy all heeded this call. Among the requested professions were makers of lager beer. Indeed, with the increased German immigration to Stevens Point, lager beer was in high demand. George Ruder and Frank Wahle were among those who sought to fill that void.

Franz, or Frank, Wahle arrived in America from Niedermarsburg, Prussia, in 1854. He first immigrated to California but returned to Europe in 1857 to marry Christina Vogt Wahle, who is pictured here. Franz and Christina traveled back to America in mid-1857 and settled in Stevens Point where Franz formed a partnership with George Ruder, who had established a brewery there. Seemingly, Wahle had no formal brewing background as his travel documents to the United States have him listed as a baker. He may have leaned on George Ruder's formal brewing background to learn the craft. After Ruder left to start his own brewery in Wausau in 1860, Wahle continued brewing with various partners until 1867, when he sold the brewery to Andrew and Jacob Lutz. Wahle then moved to Oshkosh, starting a farm and brewery there. In 1869, Wahle sold his brewery in Oshkosh, but maintained his farm, selling it months before he died in 1882. (Courtesy of Sue Bowman.)

STEVENS POIN

A. LUTZ & BROTH
STEVENS POINT, / -

George Ruder grew up in his father's brewery in Nuremberg, Bavaria. Having immigrated to Milwaukee in 1854, Ruder worked in breweries there until 1856, when he moved to Stevens Point. In Stevens Point, Ruder met Charles Ehrick, proprietor of the Plank Road House, a hotel on the road into Stevens Point. That structure is seen here on the left. It became the brewmaster's house

BREWERY.

R, PROPRIETORS.

-   -   WISCONSIN.

and the brewery storefront. Apparently, a brewery was in the early stages of construction in the lot next to the hotel when Ruder arrived in 1856. The first brewery on the grounds was constructed of wood. The stone brewery on the right was built by Andrew Lutz in 1872.

Andrew Lutz is seated front and center with his brewery employees sometime during his ownership. The gentlemen seated on the far right of the image has been used by the brewery under the name "Nicolas C. Point" and featured on tap handles and packaging. In reality, not much is known about this figure, not even his real name. This photograph was taken during the 1880s, and most records from that time have been lost.

Andrew and Jacob Lutz expanded the brewery's capacity when they constructed a new stone brewhouse in 1872. This is the oldest portion of the brewery still in existence and is still the space where beer is brewed, making the Stevens Point Brewery one of the oldest breweries with this distinction.

In 1880, Jacob Lutz left Andrew for his own brewing enterprise in nearby Grand Rapids, Wisconsin. Jacob is thought to have been the actual brewmaster in his partnership with Andrew. As such, Andrew needed someone to take over the brewing duties. He found this person in his son John. During the 1880s, the brewery began marketing itself as the Stevens Point Brewery, which can be seen branded along with Lutz's name on this beer barrel. (Both, author's collection.)

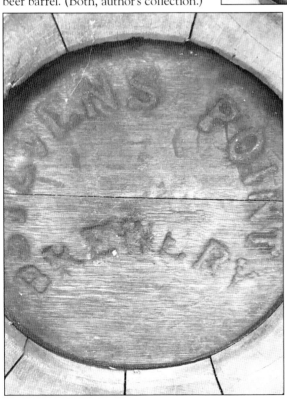

This is a Lutz beer glass from the 1880s. Items like this are very rare, as the glass is very thin and not many were produced. (Author's collection.)

Below, workers from the Lutz Brewery take a beer break in 1895. That same year, Andrew Lutz tried unsuccessfully to sell the brewery to a Milwaukee businessman, Louis Leidiger. After that deal fell through, Gustav Kuenzel purchased the brewery in 1897.

In 1880, Andrew Lutz helped his brother Jacob purchase the Schmidt Brewery in Grand Rapids. Jacob later bought the brewery from his brother. Jacob's brewery burned down in 1891. He rebuilt in 1893, constructing the Twin City Brewery, which is pictured here. That brewery was also destroyed by fire in 1895. (Courtesy of South Wood County Historical Society.)

When George Ruder left Stevens Point in 1860, he moved to Wausau and started his own brewery there. He retired from brewing in 1887, though he remained as company president. In 1892, the brewery burned to the ground. Ruder did build a new brewery in 1893, which is pictured. Unfortunately, Ruder never lived to see it as he died in December of that year. (Courtesy of the Marathon County Public Library.)

According to the German Purity Law of 1516, known as the *Reinheitsgebot*, beer traditionally contains three ingredients: barley, water, and hops. Yeast was excluded as its existence was not yet known. Portage County, where Stevens Point is located, is known historically to be a hops-producing region. This was a great benefit to local breweries such as the Stevens Point Brewery. Here, workers on Frank Guyant's farm in Belmont tend to their crop of hops in 1895. Blight in the early 1900s wiped out the commercial hops industry in Wisconsin and has yet to recover on the scale of the 19th century.

Two

INCORPORATION

After purchasing the brewery from Andrew Lutz in 1897, Gustav Kuenzel set about making his mark on the operation. He upgraded the facility in order to add more brewing capacity for his booming business. He also later changed the brewery's name to Kuenzel's to reflect his ownership. Kuezel's ownership of the brewery proved brief, however. In 1901, Michael Littel, a brewer from Green Bay, sought to buy the brewery. Needing local support and capital, Littel approached local businessmen John Martini, Nicholas Gross, and Alexander Krembs. The group successfully purchased the brewery on October 16, 1901, and immediately incorporated the brewery as the Stevens Point Brewing Company.

It was also during this era of Point Brewery that a notable competitor came on the scene, the Polish Brewing Company, which was formed in 1907. Stevens Point Brewery had encountered and defeated competition in the past from local residents like George Ellenberger, Frank Mehalsky, and Adam Kuhl. The brewery even warded off a challenge from Milwaukee's Philip Best Brewing Co., later known as Pabst. But with the large Polish population in Portage County and the sizable new Polish Brewing Company complex on nearby Wood and Wisconsin Streets, Point Brewery clearly felt threatened. So much so that they hired famed brewery architect Richard Greisser from Chicago to expand and redesign the brewery in 1907.

The Polish Brewing Company, however, encountered a string of bad luck. A cyclone leveled part of its complex in 1908. They also rebranded as the National Brewing Company in 1913, assumingly to stop being seen as only a Polish beer. The change did not enhance the company's success. The final straw came with a batch of spoiled beer in 1916. With Prohibition on the horizon, the Polish/National Brewing Company finally folded in 1917.

The Stevens Point Brewery had lasted this long due to strong management, loyal customers, and a quality product—along with a little luck—all of which would be needed to survive Prohibition.

Gustav Kuenzel purchased the brewery from Andrew Lutz in 1897. Kuenzel had worked in breweries in Germany, Austria, and Switzerland and at the Obermann Brewing Company in Milwaukee. He owned the Stevens Point Brewery until 1901. He then purchased a brewery in Hastings, Minnesota, which he ran until Prohibition took effect in 1920. Not content with producing soda and near-beer to wait out Prohibition, Kuenzel moved to Canada. There, he worked for Drewry's Brewing Company in the town of Lake of the Woods. After the repeal of Prohibition in 1933, Kuenzel accepted a job offer at the Dahlke Brewing Company, near Westfield, Wisconsin. Unfortunately, Kuenzel passed away after a brief illness in 1937. This picture is of Kuenzel during his time at Dahlke's. (Courtesy of the Marquette County Historical Society.)

While the brewery was known as the Stevens Point Brewery, Gustav Kuenzel attempted to make his own mark on the business by naming it the Kuenzel Brewing Company in 1901. This advertisement reflects that effort. Later in the year, Kuenzel sold the company to Michael Littel and his business partners, who officially changed the name to the Stevens Point Brewing Company. (Courtesy of Point Brewery.)

HAVE THE HOME BEER PURE.

WHATEVER you drink outside, let your home beer be *Kuenzel Brewing Co.* That is pure beer. Nothing in it to derange the stomach and make you bilious.

Use the beer in your home, brewed from barley and hops grown in Portage County. Beer brewed with pure, sparkling, spring water.

When you order beer for your home, get the healthfulness without the harm; get the pure beer; get the *Kuenzel Brewing Co.*

Telephone No. 61.

Kuenzel's

THE BEER THAT WILL MAKE STEVENS POINT FAMOUS.

It is thought that Gustav Kuenzel brewed a variation on Lutz's Special Beer, which would later be called Point Special Lager. He also brewed a *weissbier*, which is a German-style wheat beer. The bottle on the left is *weissbier* bottle, distinguished by its hexagonal bottom. The bottle was shaped this way to withstand the added carbonation of a *weissbier*. (Author's collection.)

Michael Littel, a brewer from Green Bay, sought to buy the brewery from Kuenzel in 1901 but needed capital to do so. With local support from men like Alexander Krembs, who is pictured here, the brewery was purchased and incorporated as the Stevens Point Brewing Company. Krembs, a local hardware merchant, served as the first brewery president.

Beer delivery certainly has changed over the years. This horse-drawn delivery wagon is seen on Third Street in downtown Stevens Point in the early 1900s.

Another Stevens Point businessman who helped Littel purchase the brewery was John Martini. Martini was born in 1859 in the Rhine Province of Germany and immigrated to Stevens Point in 1880. He first worked as a handyman, which is how he learned English. In 1885, he opened his first saloon in Stevens Point on Strongs Avenue. In 1896, he opened the luxurious Alhambra Saloon on Main Street. Martini was very active in the local business community. He was the vice president of the Stevens Point Box and Lumber Company and an investor of the Whiting Oil Company. Undoubtedly, his involvement with the Stevens Point Brewing Company related to his saloon and needing to secure product for it.

These are two different views of Main Street in Stevens Point in the 1900s. John Martini's Alhambra Saloon can be seen in the photograph above, two buildings down from the Opera House, which features a large overhang. The picture below was taken from the doorway to the Alhambra after what appears to be a large blizzard in 1909.

This is a scene from an unknown Portage County tavern in 1910. It was establishments like this that served beer from Point Brewery.

Stevens Point Brewing Co.

Largest and Best Equipped Brewery in Central Wisconsin.
BREWERS OF THE BEST QUALITY OF BEER.   Telephone 61.

With new competition from the Polish Brewing Company in 1907, Stevens Point Brewery decided to take out an advertisement in the city directory. It featured recent additions made to the facility that year.

Stevens Point Brewing Co.'s Plant, Stevens Point, Wis.

This postcard from 1910 shows just how much the brewery had expanded by that point. The stone outline in the middle of the complex is what remains of the 1872 structure built by Andrew Lutz.

This image is from a parade in Stevens Point in the early 1900s. A Stevens Point Brewing Company sign adorns the corner post of the wagon, while men nearby sip on bottles of beer.

Here, members of the Rhinae Club Band pose with a banner on a Stevens Point Brewery truck in 1908. It is interesting to note that they are standing in front of a south-side saloon that appears to be a tied house to Hagemeister Brewing from Green Bay. Hagemeister, and other out of town breweries like Pabst, tried to compete with Point Brewery with little success.

In the early days of Point Brewery, workers would harvest ice in the winter at McDill pond and then store it in an icehouse. It must have been a big deal then when the brewery installed mechanical refrigeration in 1908. The refrigeration equipment is seen here with brewery workers posing in front of it during the 1910s.

George Egenhoefer (right) was born in Hoechstadt, Germany, in 1863. He studied brewing there before moving to America in 1892. Upon his arrival, he worked in Baltimore before being hired as brewmaster of the Stevens Point Brewery in 1912. It was reported in the *Stevens Point Journal* in 1939 that Egenhoefer was the oldest active brewmaster in the United States at 75 years old.

This picture shows brewmaster George Egenhoefer (left) with brewery workers and local townspeople posing on top of a delivery truck fully stocked with wooden beer barrels.

A brewery worker stands by the machinery and equipment of the steam-powered engine room in the 1910s.

By 1910, more than 20 full-time employees staffed the brewery, with extra help being brought in during busier times of the year.

In the 1910s, the brewery bottle shop was still housed in the former Plank Road House, the first structure on the property in 1856. The building, which also served as the brewmaster's house, remained on site until it was torn down in the 1950s to make way for a new brewmaster's house.

The Stevens Point Brewery featured two products named after brewery treasurer and plant manager Nicholas "Pinky" Gross: Pink's Pale and Pink's Crystal. Gross worked for Milwaukee's Philip Best Brewing Company and later the Pabst Brewing Company before joining the syndicate that bought and incorporated Point Brewery. He worked as brewery manager until 1924. He was 72 years old when he died in 1926. (Author's collection.)

Roll out the barrel! Brewery workers pose in the keg filling area of the brewery in the late 1910s. Wooden kegs were sealed with pitch to prevent leakage before being filled with beer. Wooden kegs were used by the brewery until the 1950s.

By 1910, Point Brewery had grown considerably from its modest roots established by Ruder, Wahle, and the Lutz family. While the structure constructed by Andrew Lutz is clearly visible in the center of the building, note that the facility had more than tripled in size by this point.

In 1914, the brewery moved the original brewmaster's house and bottle shop around the corner, from Water Street to Francis Street. This was to make way for a modern office and bottling facility. This structure remains today as the brewery's gift shop. Meanwhile, there are offices where the trees are to the left of the building.

The Fourth of July has long been a reason for celebration in Stevens Point. Races, concerts, and, of course, fireworks have dotted itineraries for Independence Day festivities going back to the early days of the city. This is a picture of one such gathering on the south side of Stevens Point in 1910. Note the Point Brewery advertisement on the building behind the stage.

The Polish Brewing Company had limited success compared to the more established Stevens Point Brewing Company. Polish Brewing renamed itself as National Brewing in attempt at rebranding in 1913, however, a batch of spoiled beer in 1916 finished the brewery for good. The building was later bought by the Bake-rite Bread Company, which remained there until the structure was torn down in the 1990s.

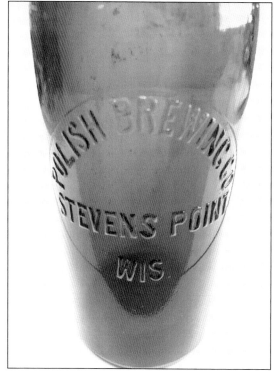

A brutal cyclone ripped through Stevens Point in November 1908. Several city blocks south of downtown were damaged or destroyed. One of the casualties was the Polish Brewing Company. While they did rebuild, it was the first in a series of mishaps that ultimately doomed the brewery.

Many prominent Stevens Point businessmen were involved in the Polish Brewing Company. Joseph and Anton Firkus, Michael Bannach, and John Zynda were among its board members. John Bukolt, founder of the Lullabye Furniture Company, was also among its investors. The Polish Brewing Company represents the last major local competitor for Point Brewery in Stevens Point. (Author's collection.)

Three

SURVIVAL

Prohibition forced many breweries to close. Those that chose to stay in business converted their facilities for other uses. The Stevens Point Brewery decided to try to wait Prohibition out by making soda and near-beer. For soda, the brewery became a bottling franchise for Coca-Cola and manufactured a variety of their own flavors. The brewery also produced nonalcoholic beer (less than .5 percent alcohol) with Nubru, Malt Tonic, Heavy Dark Brew, and Point Special Beverage.

As the brewery was struggling through Prohibition, a brewery supply salesman from Milwaukee, Ludwig Korfmann, began inquiring about buying stock in the company. Korfmann was familiar with the Stevens Point area because Portage County once was a large producer of one of beer's central ingredients, hops. As management grew weary of battling Prohibition, Korfmann purchased a controlling interest in the brewery on February 29, 1924. As Prohibition had forced the brewery to make non-beer products, Korfmann renamed the company the Stevens Point Beverage Company.

By 1929, Korfmann began predicting the end of Prohibition. He would bet "his hat" to anyone who would listen to him that Prohibition would end that year. Korfmann ended up losing three hats. By 1932, with the election of Franklin D. Roosevelt and his campaign promise of repealing Prohibition, Korfmann's prediction finally became a reality. At midnight on April 7, 1933, the first keg of Point Special Beer was consumed in less than an hour at the Congress Club in Stevens Point. By morning, cars were lined up down the street waiting to take home bottles of Point Beer. The brewery worked around the clock for two weeks to keep up with demand.

The challenges did not subside for the brewery post-Prohibition, however. World War II forced material and ingredient rationing on the brewery. Meanwhile, large breweries were consolidating smaller entities to strengthen their own market share as a defensive measure in the event that Prohibition returned. Ludwig Korfmann passed away in 1941, leaving the company to his son Calvin. Calvin's steady ownership and the loyalty of the community ultimately kept the brewery afloat during these difficult times in the industry.

When Prohibition went into effect in 1920, many breweries went out of business. The Stevens Point Brewery remained intact by producing near-beer. Many stockholders grew weary with the decline in revenue. Ludwig Korfmann (left) decided to hedge his bets on the brewery and bought their shares, purchasing controlling interest in 1924. He rebranded the brewery as the Stevens Point Beverage Company. Here, Korfmann is pictured with brewmaster George Egenhoefer.

Point Special, a name with its roots in the Lutz era of the brewery, was resurrected during Prohibition for the brewery's near-beer. To create near-beer, the brewery first made regular beer and then essentially boiled the alcohol out to make it a legal beverage. After Prohibition, the brewery kept the label and simply changed the word "beverage" to "beer."

SOMETHING NEW

POINT SPECIAL

A Malt Beverage, brewed from choice malt and imported hops. Fully fermented, and aged in glass enameled casks. Tastes like pre-war lager. Brewed and bottled by

Stevens Point Beverage Co.

Phone 61   "A Home Industry"

This is an advertisement from 1929 for Point Special Beverage. It is interesting that by this point in Prohibition, the company had dropped the phrase "non-intoxicating" from its marketing. Previously, the brewery did include that phrase to show compliance for the Prohibition laws.

Superior Quality

CHERRY SODA

CONTENTS 24 FL. OZ.

BOTTLED BY
STEVENS POINT BEVERAGE CO.

During Prohibition, Point Brewery changed its name to Stevens Point Beverage Company and started producing soft drinks. Notably, it was contracted to make Purple and Orange Crush for Coca-Cola, among other flavors of that company's own soda.

Charles Schenk was born in 1862 in Portage, Wisconsin, to German immigrant parents. He moved to Stevens Point in the 1880s and first worked as a barber. In 1889, he opened a jewelry store on Main Street with his brother-in-law. He was elected as Stevens Point city treasurer in 1895. He left that post when the Stevens Point Brewing Company incorporated in 1901, becoming treasurer of the brewery. After Nicholas Gross retired in 1924, Schenk became manager of the brewery, holding that job until his death in 1943 at the age of 81.

By 1931, Prohibition had taken a large toll on the Stevens Point Brewery. Two years prior, the brewery had stopped making beer entirely, even near-beer, focusing solely on soda production. Production of Point Special Beverage was contracted out to another brewery, who then shipped it back to Point Brewery to be bottled. That said, the brewery was optimistic that Prohibition would end. It started updating brewing equipment in 1931 with the hope that the law would change soon.

Prohibition also decimated the workforce for Point Brewery. In 1916, four years before Prohibition, the brewery employed 24 men. By 1931, only five employees remained, including office staff. These pictures show the brewery and brewmaster's house prior to the post-Prohibition sales surge that would save the company.

Prohibition was a tough time for all breweries, including Stevens Point. Many went out of business. It was a cause for great celebration when, in 1936, the brewery made enough money to issue bonus checks to employees. Workers pose here with their first post-repeal bonus checks. Brewery owner Ludwig Korfmann is the figure in the center in the lighter-colored suit.

This an advertisement with the rules for naming "Prize Beer" in 1939. Note that entrants must send in seven Prize Beer labels in order to enter. It was a clever marketing scheme to get the community to try the new beer. It was also a test by the brewery to see if the local market could support two products from the same brewery.

Hundreds of entries were submitted to name the new Prize Beer. Here, brewery manager Charles Schenk is pouring over some of the suggestions.

Here is a suggestion from Stevens Point resident Herman Ash to call the Prize Beer "Point Badger." Obviously, Ash did not take first prize, as the winning entry was called "Amber Prize." It is unknown who submitted the grand prize–winning name.

Please enter the following name in your "Prize Beer" contest:

"POINT BADGER"

I bought my Prize Beer from George Woryalla at "club 10".

HERMAN E. ASH
HIGHBANKS COTTAGE
PHONE 543 R4
MAIL ADDRESS: P.O. Box 163
STEVENS POINT, WIS.

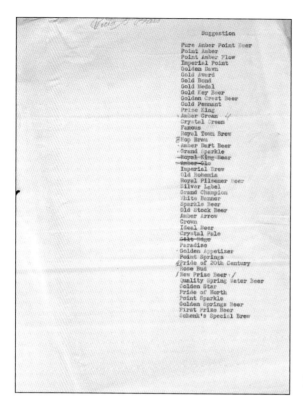

Suggestion
Pure Amber Point Beer
Point Amber
Point Amber Flow
Imperial Point
Golden Dawn
Gold Award
Gold Bond
Gold Medal
Gold Key Beer
Golden Crest Beer
Gold Pennant
Prize King
Amber Cream
Crystal Cream
Famous
Royal Town Brew
Hop Brau
Amber Dart Beer
Grand Sparkle
Royal King Beer
Amber Glo
Imperial Brew
Old Bohemia
Royal Pilsener Beer
Silver Label
Grand Champion
White Banner
Sparkle Beer
Old Stock Beer
Amber Arrow
Crown
Ideal Beer
Crystal Pale
Salt Lake
Paradise
Golden Appetizer
Point Springs
Pride of 20th Century
Rose Bud
New Prize Beer
Quality Spring Water Beer
Golden Star
Pride of North
Point Sparkle
Golden Springs Beer
First Prize Beer
Schenk's Special Brew

This is a collection of Prize Beer naming entries as viewed by the brewery. It is interesting to note "Point Amber" near the top of the list. A beer by that name would come out in the 1990s.

In the end, the winner of the Prize Beer contest was Amber Prize. It is unknown if a single entry was made with this name or if the brewery had the name all along but came up with the contest as a marketing stunt. In any case, Amber Prize was short-lived. The beer was discontinued at the outbreak of World War II due to rationing.

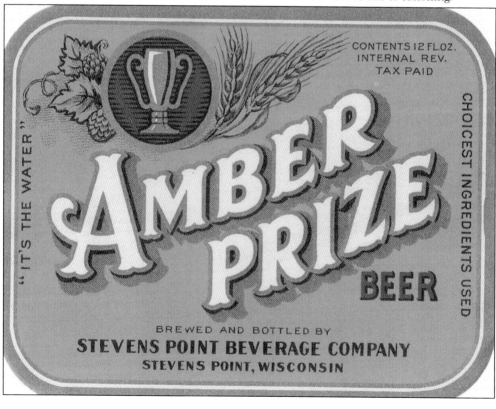

When Ludwig Korfmann passed away in 1941, his son Calvin took over as president of the brewery. Calvin had served as secretary of the brewery since his father's purchase of the plant in 1924. Calvin Korfmann would hold the post of president until 1970.

Felix "Phil" Shibilski was hired by the brewery as an accountant in 1930. With Prohibition-era staffing reductions in force at the brewery, he had a wide range of tasks to tend to. Shibilski's early duties included keeping the books, delivering product, and testing the product for quality control. After Charles Schenk died in 1943, Shibilski was promoted to brewery manager.

Since the brewery's founding in the 1850s, the buildings have seen many renovations and upgrades. Here, workers put bricks in the windows that were no longer needed from the earlier days of the brewery.

Wooden aging tanks were lined with a resin to prevent leakage of the beer and maintain flavor.

Here is the brewery as is looked in 1937. In that year, another major addition was made to the brewery when a large garage was constructed on the property, which can be seen in the bottom right of both pictures.

When Prohibition ended, new laws dictated that beer brands be clearly marked when served at a tavern. Thus, the tap handle industry was born. Early tap handles were small, like the one pictured, and known as "ball tap knobs." This example is from Point Brewery in the 1930s. (Courtesy of Kevin Knitt.)

Big Charlie was a huge 64-ounce "picnic beer" filled with Point Special. Like Amber Prize, Big Charlie was also discontinued during World War II as the large bottles were inefficient to package and ship. The name "Big Charlie" is a reference to longtime brewery manager Charles Schenk.

One task that must be completed often in brewing is cleaning. These pictures show a Point Brewery worker scrubbing the floors of the brewhouse in the 1950s.

A worker services the bottling line in the 1940s.

These are Point Beer bottles from the 1950s. While Point Special has been the flagship beer for the brewery since Prohibition, the brewery's seasonal Point Bock has also been popular over the years. While the brewery did discontinue Point Bock during World War II, it brought it back in 1946, making it the only product to make a postwar return. (Author's collection.)

Ed Kurz was hired as brewmaster in 1944. Kurz had learned how to brew beer at Tivoli Brewing Company in Detroit, where his father-in-law was the brewmaster. Kurz moved to southeastern Wisconsin for a brewmaster job in 1944 but found that the brewery had mafia connections. Fortunately, the Stevens Point Brewery was in need of a brewmaster, and Kurz was hired.

This is a photograph of the brewery in 1950. The brewery ran advertisements around this time that recommended that customers keep a case or two of Point Special on hand at all times. Promotional efforts also included the sponsoring of Ed Hansen's Point Special Sports Broadcast on local radio station WFHR.

This 1950s delivery fleet is ready to make sure area retailers and establishments are stocked with the hometown product. Seeing one of these rigs rolling down the road would have certainly been a welcome sight. Drivers are, from left to right, Larry Konopacki, Clarence Check, Jim Spreda, Vic Marshall, Mike Mansavage, Wally Przybylski, George Grubba, Bernie Yach, and Lenny Chistenson.

Calvin Korfmann was the life of the party! Not only was the brewery owner good at selling beer, he also played drums. While it is unknown what style of music the band is playing in this photograph, if it was taken near Stevens Point, it would undoubtedly be a polka.

Mike Mansavage is shown here with his delivery truck. Mansavage started working at the brewery right after Prohibition in 1933 and worked there for 33 years, retiring in 1976.

The 1950s were an era of growth and evolution for Point Brewery. In 1953, the brewery started canning its beer for the first time. Point Brewery was late to this industry trend as beer was first canned in 1935 by the Krueger Brewing Company of Newark, New Jersey. While larger breweries started canning not long after, it took smaller operations like Point longer to adapt because the new equipment was a significant investment.

These kegs are waiting to be filled with delicious Point Beer. This version is called a Hoff-Stevens keg. This is the version of the keg that came between wooden barrels and the modern Sankey keg.

Here, a worker conducts quality control on the bottling line. He is ensuring that every bottle contains the same amount of beer, with no particles or contamination inside.

This is a 1950s advertisement that showcases the range of packaging options for Point Special. Sizes ranged from the seven-ounce "Pointer" bottles to large quart-sized bottles.

A delivery of Point Beer was indeed a "special delivery." These two pictures show the variation on small-order delivery trucks from the 1940s to the 1970s.

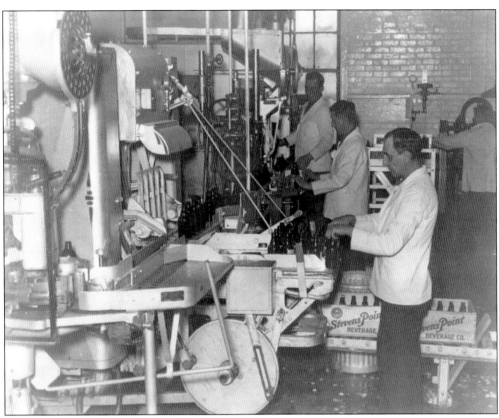

After returnable bottles were brought back to the brewery, the bottles needed to be cleaned before they were filled and capped again. Here, brewery workers tend to the bottle-cleaning machines.

Here is Mike Witkowski at work in the brewhouse, with the brew kettle behind him. Witkowski worked at the brewery for 42 years, retiring in 1982.

This is the magical moment where the bottles and the case meet. A 1950s brewery worker makes sure that another case of Point Special leaves the bottling line intact.

This is a picture of the brewery in the winter of 1956. There is a railcar parked on the side of the building. Brewery supplies and ingredients used to be delivered by train. Remnants of the train tracks still exist in the parking lot across the street from the brewery.

This is a brewery display from a trade show in the 1950s. Featured at the center of the display is a sign reading, "BRAVES." Point Brewery was a local sponsor of the Milwaukee Braves baseball team in the late 1950s.

This is a 1955 picture of the brewery taken from the field across the street. The brewery at this time produced 40,000 barrels of beer a year.

This billboard welcomed residents and visitors alike with the advertisement of hometown beer. The water quality in Stevens Point is some of the best in the country, a fact prominently displayed on the billboard.

When Stevens Point celebrated its centennial in 1958, a huge party and parade were thrown on Main Street, and Point Brewery brought the beer. Here, the Point Brewery float cruises down Main Street.

A cart of Stevens Point's finest products are ready to be loaded on an airplane bound for an exhibit in Washington, DC, around 1960. Pork, potatoes, and Point Beer all made the trip.

In the photograph at right, Phil Shibilski (second from left), Calvin Korfmann (third from left), and others help load a plane with Point Special cases for the Wisconsin exhibit in Washington, DC. This marks the first time any Point Brewery products were sent out of state.

The Wisconsin exhibit in Washington, DC, prominently featured the state's brewing industry. The patron saint of beer, King Gambrinus, and a short history of the beverage are shown here.

This section of the Wisconsin brewing exhibit shows the different breweries throughout the state. While there were still dozens of breweries in Wisconsin in 1960, by 1975 only a handful remained, with Point Brewery among them.

Here, Point Special is being enjoyed by two famous Central Wisconsin residents. Melvin Laird (left) served as a congressman from 1953 to 1969 and then as secretary of defense until 1973. On the right is K.B. Willet, a leader in the Stevens Point community through numerous causes. He was so dedicated to the city that he earned the nickname "Mr. Stevens Point."

Another shipment of Point Beer is about to be on its way to loyal customers. This photograph was taken in the 1960s.

Brewery tours are not a new event. Here, guests are being shown beer that is fermenting in 1965.

The crew at Journal Printing in Stevens Point enjoy an after-work Point Special in 1960. From left to right are (seated) Bob Czalplinski; (standing) Ben Glennon, Dale Werner, Dave Menske, Ed Kryshak, and Erv Lepak. (Courtesy of Point Brewery.)

While Ed Kurz was from Milwaukee, he was not from a brewing family. His father was a city architect. Kurz spent his high school summers working for Schlitz Brewing and learned of the brewing profession through his father-in-law, Gunther Schmidt. Schmidt worked at Tivoli Brewing in Detroit, where Kurz apprenticed. Kurz was also educated at the US Brewing Academy in New York.

This picture shows brewmaster Ed Kurz (left) with chief engineer Leo Repinski (right) in front of the keg-filling machine in the 1960s. Repinski was employed by the brewery for 30 years.

These are Kurz family photographs from their time living in the brewmaster's house next to the brewery. Ed Kurz's wife, Bertha, is seen here with the rest of the family. The brewmaster's house was the same Plank Road house that existed on the property since 1856 and was fairly rundown by that time. In the mid-1950s, the brewery built a new brewmaster's house, which remained on the premises until the 1990s, when it was moved down the block. Kurz's son Andy said that there was also always Point Special in the house, which became much more appreciated as he reached his teenage years.

Calvin Korfmann remained as brewery president until 1970, when he handed the operation over to Phil Shibilski. Korfmann was a major contributor to the local Stevens Point community. He was a trustee for the Stevens Point YMCA and a director of the Stevens Point Area Health Foundation. He was very engaged with the brewing industry, serving as treasurer for the Wisconsin State Brewers Association. He was also a director of the US Brewers Association. He passed away in 1974 at the age of 76.

This is a 1960s picture of brewery workers on the bottling line.

By 1970, the brewery was one of only 14 left in the state. While that number continued to decrease, the Stevens Point Brewery always found a way to survive.

Calvin Korfmann donated the land across the street from the brewery as a Little League Baseball field. He also built dugouts and a scoreboard for the field. Here, Korfmann (right) is seen with Len Debaker (left) of the First National Bank of Stevens Point unveiling the new ball field.

A swing and a miss! Two Little League teams face off at the newly completed Korfmann Field, across the street from Point Brewery in 1966. The field would later be turned into event ground for the Rock the Brewery concert series and Pointoberfest celebrations.

This is an aerial shot of the brewery from 1968. The Little League field is visible across the street.

In the late 1960s, a distributor for Schlitz Brewing from Milwaukee predicted the downfall of the small, regional Stevens Point Brewery. Phil Shibilski replied, "We'll be here longer than Schlitz will be in Milwaukee." Shibilski was proved right, as Schlitz closed its Milwaukee operations in 1982 and Point Brewery has lasted over 160 years.

Downtown on the square was, and still is, the place to be for nightlife. Taverns have been located on the square since the early days of Stevens Point. This photograph from the 1960s shows that Beanie's Memorial Pub is proudly serving the hometown beer, Point Special.

As the 1970s began, the challenges were large for the venerable Point Brewery. It would take more of the same consistent quality product—and a little luck—for the brewery to survive into the future.

Four

THE BEST BEER
IN AMERICA

It was a tough business being a small, regional brewery in the early 1970s. The big breweries such as Miller, Schlitz, and Budweiser could beat the smaller breweries on price due to their large volume of sales. The smaller breweries, in turn, would have to lower their prices to compete but could not keep their profit margins. Many breweries had their equipment fall into disrepair, as they did not have money for maintenance. Others would turn to cheaper ingredients, which, of course, made lower-quality beer, which led to less sales. This would turn into a vicious cycle that would end when the brewery either closed or was bought out by a larger competitor. The effect this trend had on the American brewing industry was devastating. At the end of Prohibition in 1933, there were 750 breweries nationwide. By 1973, there were only 65.

It was looking as though Point Brewery could be caught in this downturn as well until the brewery got an unexpected boost from an unlikely source: a newspaper columnist in Chicago named Mike Royko. In a May 22, 1973, column, Royko wrote that American beer tasted as if the "brewing process involved running it through a horse." Royko experienced swift backlash after this comment from readers who were angry that he attacked their beer. Royko responded by holding a blind taste test. The winner was Wurzberger, a pilsner from Germany. The surprise came with the second-place winner and the top American beer in the taste test: Point Special.

No one is even sure how a case of Point Special made it to Chicago. At the time, Point's distribution radius was only about 50 miles. Rumor has it that brewmaster Ed Kurz snuck a case to Royko against the wishes of brewery management, who did not want to partake in such antics. Or perhaps Royko picked up a case while visiting his father who lived in nearby Mosinee. Whatever the case may be, Royko's article made Point Special the number one American beer and gave the brewery new life.

The year 1973 was shaping up to be a year of grand recognition for Point Brewery. In January of that year, the brewery was presented with the International Oktoberfest Award from the Brewer's Association of America. Phil Shibilski (left) and Ed Kurz are seen here holding the award.

In the early 1970s, the saying "When you're out of Point, you're out of town" was meant literally. The brewery only distributed within a 50-mile radius of Stevens Point. If someone wanted to buy Point Beer, they needed to be in or near Stevens Point.

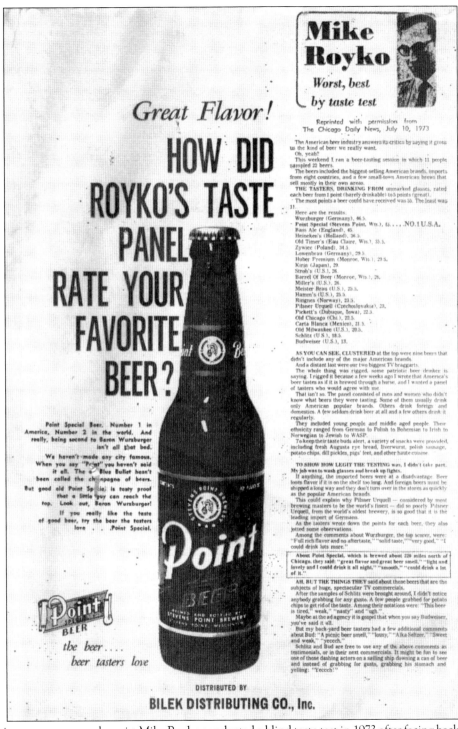

Chicago newspaper columnist Mike Royko conducted a blind taste test in 1973 after facing backlash for making disparaging comments about American beer. While most of those comments were proved correct in the taste test, with Budweiser and Schlitz landing toward the bottom, Point Special was ranked second in the world and first in America.

WHEN YOU'RE NUMBER ONE,
THERE MUST BE A REASON

Being ranked as the number one beer in America by a nationwide taste test provided the marketing opportunity that the brewery needed to survive the era of mass consolidation in the brewing industry. People from around the country journeyed to Stevens Point to taste Point Special. Point Brewery rolled out advertisements like these to tout its newfound claim to greatness. (Both, courtesy of Point Brewery.)

Indeed, locals took pride in the attention that the brewery was receiving from the taste test. Even as orders came in from as far away as Colorado or as big as several hundred cases a week from Trans World Airlines (TWA), the brewery kept its focus on the local market. This loyalty was reciprocated by the residents of Stevens Point. This picture was taken at the 1974 Portage County Fair in Rosholt, Wisconsin.

Future brewery president and owner Ken Shibilski, second from right, chats with workers near the case filling machine in the early 1970s.

This picture shows brewery workers rolling finished cases down the line. Stacks of Point Special surround them, waiting to be distributed.

This is a top view of the brew kettle in the brewhouse at Point Brewery. It is at this stage in the brewing process that hops bitter the sweet liquid known at wort before the yeast is added for fermentation.

This photograph shows bottles being pasteurized after they are filled with beer. The pasteurization process kills any lingering bacteria in the beer. Pasteurizing beer extends its shelf life by several months.

This is an art proof used by the Point Brewery marketing team in the mid-1970s. The advertisement focuses on how being smaller and more local is better. These are two aspects that helped the brewery as the industry shifted toward craft brewing in the 1990s and 2000s.

Even the animals drink Point Special in Stevens Point. One of these piglets is certainly being a hog by not letting the runt in the back get to its bottle of the local brew.

After the Royko contest declared Point Special the best beer in America, the brewery had a big reason to update its marketing to reflect that distinction. Even the delivery trucks were painted with "#1 USA."

These are the men behind the number one beer in America in 1973. From left to right are brewery president Phil Shibilski, assistant manager Ken Shibilski, and brewmaster Ed Kurz. Kurz retired in 1977 after 33 years with the brewery.

These pictures are from when a group of local sportswriters partnered with the brewery for fans to win Point Beer T-shirts in 1975. At right are, from left to right, (first row) Ken Shibilski and Gil Molski from Point Brewery; (second row) Mike Haberman, Randy Wievel, and Tim Sullivan. They are in front of the prominent Water Street and Beer Street signs that existed until the brewery expanded in the 2000s. The image below was taken outside the brewery's hospitality room.

This is how a 24 pack of Point Special cans was packaged in 1974. The packaging changed as the brewery converted to aluminum cans in the 1980s.

Point Special was a welcome sight for Stevens Point native George Hanson while he was stationed in Vietnam in 1970 and 1971. His wife, Joanie, sent him cans of Point Beer three times during his service by sneaking it into care packages. Hanson would refer to Point Special as "the nectar of the gods."

These photographs show two generations of Point Special can packaging. The image above shows the steel cans which existed from 1953 until 1982. The photograph below shows the "new" aluminum cans in 1982. Aluminum cans are lighter and more environmentally friendly. Customers also said that the beer tasted better out of aluminum cans.

In the 1970s, the time came to upgrade some of the brewery's equipment. The old wooden aging, or lagering, tanks were upgraded to steel vessels. This photograph shows the removed tanks with a curious neighborhood child.

This image shows a combination of old and new brewery aging tanks. The old wooden aging tank on the right was being replaced by the steel tank at left in the 1970s.

The above photograph shows the Point Special packaging lineup in the early 1970s, while the image below shows the Point Special lineup in 1983. The small seven-ounce Pointer as well as the large 32-ounce version of the product were eventually phased out.

Point Brewery converted from steel to aluminum cans in 1982. Here, cans of Point Special receive their lids on the canning line. The brewery spent $125,000 to switch from steel to aluminum canning. That money was earned back through lower shipping costs.

To keep the machinery in top condition, regular cleaning and maintenance had to be conducted. Here, a brewery worker cleans the canning line.

Here, Phil (left) and Ken (right) Shibilski enjoy a fresh Point Special in the brewery's hospitality room in 1982. The Shibilskis created a grand legacy with the brewery, as either Phil or Ken was involved with operations from 1930 to the mid-1990s.

Before the modern taproom was installed at Point Brewery, tours ended in the hospitality room. This is also the room where company Christmas parties and gatherings took place.

This photograph is from the 1982 company Christmas party with members of staff and management enjoying a Point Special. From left to right are Diane Sankey, Jim Landry, Ken Shibilski, Phil Shibilski, Tom Thompson, and John Zappa.

These three men were in charge of three big names in brewing in Wisconsin. From left to right are Ken Shibilski, of Point Brewery; Chuck Walter, of Walter's Brewing in Eau Claire; and Bill Leinenkugel, of Leinenkugel's Brewing in Chippewa Falls. They posed for this photograph at the 1982 State Wholesalers Convention. (Courtesy of Point Brewery.)

Another person responsible for Point Brewery's consistent growth was sales manager Tom Thompson. Thompson, left, is seen here with Ken Shibilski at the 1982 State Wholesalers Convention. (Courtesy of Point Brewery.)

Three men from Kellner proudly fly a Point Beer flag at their campground near Mole Lake in Northern Wisconsin in 1982. (Both, courtesy of Point Brewery)

Brewery worker Connie Lepak is shown here loading cases of Point Special cans into a delivery truck in the 1980s.

The brewery used reusable bottles into the late 2000s. This 1980s photograph shows a worker unloading cases of empties to be put back into service once again.

Brewery worker Joe Nachman loads and inspects a pallet of Point Special cans for delivery in 1989.

Art Oksuita (right) joined the brewery in 1978 as a maintenance engineer. His predecessor basically gave him a two-hour tour of the brewery before Oksuita was on his own to make sure the brewery kept running, and he did that job so thoroughly, he was eventually promoted to the position of director of operations. From left to right are Tom Thompson, Diane Sankey, Ken Shibilski, John Zappa, Jim Landry, and Oksuita.

John Zappa joined Point Brewery as brewmaster in 1977, when Ed Kurz retired. Zappa had previously worked for Grain Belt Brewing in Minneapolis and Schmidt Brewing in St. Paul. A huge upgrade was made in 1985 when the brewery installed new brewhouse equipment. This investment in top-of-the-line brewing equipment ensured that Point Brewery would remain competitive into the craft beer era. In this photograph, Zappa inspects the new brew kettle.

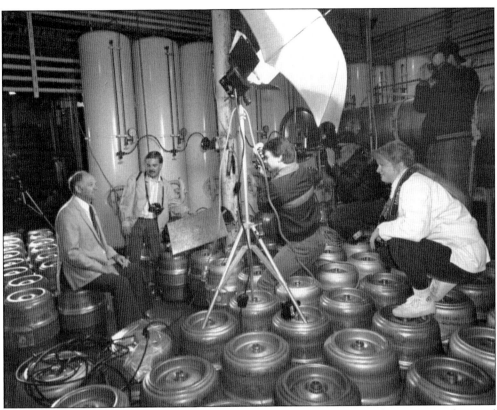

Running a small, successful brewery was a big deal in the 1980s. Here, brewery president and owner Ken Shibilski poses for photographs in front of the brewery and in the keg room.

Here, Ken Shibilski (in a coat and tie) gives a tour to show off the brand-new brewhouse equipment in 1985. While the brewhouse equipment was all new, the brewery still employed some of the wooden aging tanks, as seen below.

In 1985, Point Brewery launched a new product: Eagle Premium Pilsner. The beer was billed as a lighter, smoother-tasting premium beer. The beer was supposedly a throwback to a George Egenhoefer recipe known as Eagles Special that was brewed in the 1910s before Prohibition. (Both, courtesy of Pat Shibilski.)

This is a photograph of the installation of new fermenting tanks at the brewery in 1989. The purpose of adding these tanks was to enlarge brewing capacity so the brewery could focus on more specialty beers, as the brewery was transitioning to a more craft-like operation.

Point Light's logo is featured in the bottom corner of this photograph. The brewery started making Point Light in 1988 but encountered major light-beer competition from Miller and Budweiser. After trying different improvements on the recipe with no added success, the brewery phased the product out of its portfolio in the 2000s.

Point Beer has long been a favorite of locals at community gatherings. In this photograph, Stevens Point resident Gary Klonowski enjoys a Point Special at an event in the 1980s.

By 1990, the beer industry had changed significantly for regional breweries. As the giants like Miller and Budweiser still dominated market share, new craft breweries were popping up all over the country. Point Brewery's ability to compete with both extremes in the industry is another reason for its continued success.

As the early 1990s arrived, so did another update in packaging for Point Special. A deer was featured at the top of the logo as new marketing encouraged customers to "Score a few Points tonight."

Five

THE NEXT CHAPTER

In 1990, Point Brewery sold beer outside of the state of Wisconsin for the first time in the brewery's history. This growth in consumer demand led president and owner Ken Shibilski to sell the brewery to Chicago-based Barton Beers in 1992. Shibilski, who was eying retirement and other ventures, sold in order to make sure that new capital was injected into the brewery. Barton Beers was a large brewing conglomerate with many different brands in its portfolio, namely Corona. Barton's ownership marked a time of updating equipment and marketing in order to strengthen Point Brewery for the future. Among the improvements made by Barton was the addition of new aging tanks in 1994, which increased brewing capacity by 40 percent. Barton also built a new 15,000-square-foot warehouse to keep up with shipping operations.

As the craft beer movement was gaining momentum, the brewery caught the eye of two Milwaukee businessmen: Jim Weichmann and his business partner Joe Martino. In 2002, they bought the brewery, returning the operation to Wisconsin ownership. Weichmann and Martino wasted no time in putting their mark on the brewery legacy, launching Point Premium Root Beer in 2002, followed by three more gourmet sodas in 2005. They have also invested millions of dollars in new packaging and equipment, ensuring the brewery's viability for years to come.

The brewery has also expanded its beer offerings, making it a true craft brewery. Along with seasonal beers and limited releases, the brewery also launched a premium beer brand, Whole Hog, in 2009 and Cider Boys hard ciders in 2012. Point Brewery has expanded its distribution across the country, and Point Special continues to win medals at major beer festivals. With all of these changes occurring in the brewing business, Point Brewery has not lost sight of its history. Point Special is still the beer one finds on tap at most taverns in Stevens Point and still the beer that locals are proud to put their name on.

This 1992 document features many of Point Special's package designs over the years. The marketing department used documents to test out designs, concepts, and fonts.

Brewmaster John Zappa is seen here in the center with people modeling a new line of Point Brewery merchandise for the cover of its 1990 catalog.

It has long been publicized that Stevens Point has some of the best water quality in the country. In the 1990s, this claim was put to the test as a national water-quality group came to Stevens Point. Brewmaster John Zappa is seen here sampling the water himself at a tasting event held at the brewery.

Here, brewery employee Tom Printz works the controls of the canning line.

The introduction of Point Amber into the marketplace had more to do with sausage than beer. In the early 1990s, Johnsonville Sausage Co. was looking for a beer to make its bratwurst with. Point Brewery sent samples of a medium-bodied amber lager to Johnsonville, which ultimately was chosen as the beer it would use. During this process, the brewery realized it had created a flavorsome beer, which it decided to market on its own. (Both, courtesy of Point Brewery.)

The brewery always makes for a great photo op for a wedding party. These newlyweds and their wedding party made sure a stop at Point Brewery was included on their wedding day. (Courtesy of Point Brewery.)

From 2003 to 2007, the baseball field across the street from the brewery became the site of a major concert series: Rock the Brewery. Artists such as Cheap Trick, REO Speedwagon, Night Ranger, Loverboy, and many others took the stage during the festivities. (Courtesy of Point Brewery.)

In 1992, the brewery was sold to Barton Beers, Inc., from Chicago. This allowed for more marketing dollars to be funneled to the brewery, leading to a larger out of state presence. Barton also made significant investments in facility upgrades. As Barton was then also purchased by a larger conglomerate, two Milwaukee businessmen saw an opportunity to bring the brewery back under Wisconsin ownership.

Milwaukeeans Jim Weichmann and Joe Martino purchased the brewery in 2002. Expanding to keep up with industry trends has been a top priority for them. The brewery has not only launched a gourmet soda line in 2002, but also continues to align itself with the craft beer boom by releasing small-batch beers and seasonal offerings beyond the flagship Point Special brand.

Part of the expansion plan for the brewery was to fill in the courtyard space between the brewhouse and the bottling and office space. Where railcars used to drop off and pick up brewing supplies and beer is now where fermenting tanks exist. This is the brewery as it stands in 2019.

Many taverns in Stevens Point feature signage from the hometown brewery, like this one outside of the Elbow Room on the Public Square. The Elbow Room's claim to fame is that its structure is believed to be the oldest saloon building in Stevens Point; it was constructed in 1890 by John Nowak and still functions as a saloon. (Author's collection.)

In 2017, Point Brewery and local arts organization CREATE Portage County constructed a mural on Clark Street in downtown Stevens Point. The mural painter was Chicago-based artist Nick Goettling, who stated, "I want to inspire the people who live there and visitors alike to really think about the decades of locally-grown knowledge, skills, and ingredients that go into a pint of Stevens Point Beer. It's nodding to the past while looking forward." (Author's collection.)

ABOUT THE ORGANIZATION

The Portage County Historical Society's goal is to preserve the unique history of this county and to present a variety of programs to bring that unique history and heritage to both residents and visitors. These programs include (among others) speakers, museum displays, and assistance with individual's requests for research. The society operates four sites around the county: the Beth Israel Synagogue, Fire House No. 2, Nelsonville Mill, and Heritage Park in Plover.

The Portage County Historical Society also houses much of its valuable archival collection at the University of Wisconsin–Stevens Point's archives. Without these collections, this book would not have been possible. The author is sincerely grateful for these stewards of historical knowledge for preserving the past so well.

DISCOVER THOUSANDS OF LOCAL HISTORY BOOKS FEATURING MILLIONS OF VINTAGE IMAGES

Arcadia Publishing, the leading local history publisher in the United States, is committed to making history accessible and meaningful through publishing books that celebrate and preserve the heritage of America's people and places.

Find more books like this at
www.arcadiapublishing.com

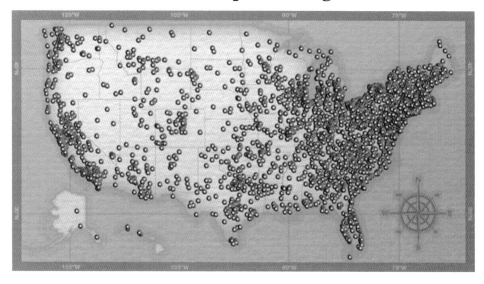

Search for your hometown history, your old stomping grounds, and even your favorite sports team.